# Celebrating Earth Day

BY M. J. YORK

**The Child's World®**
childsworld.com

Published by The Child's World®
1980 Lookout Drive • Mankato, MN 56003-1705
800-599-READ • www.childsworld.com

Photographs ©: Paula Photo/Shutterstock Images, cover,
1; Tinna Pong/Shutterstock Images, 5; Susan Chiang/
iStockphoto, 6–7; Liquidlibrary/Thinkstock, 8; Monkey
Business Images/Shutterstock Images, 11, 20–21;
Shutterstock Images, 13, 16–17, 18; Wavebreakmedia/
Shutterstock Images, 14

Design Element: Shutterstock Images

Copyright © 2017 by The Child's World®
All rights reserved. No part of this book may be
reproduced or utilized in any form or by any means
without written permission from the publisher.

ISBN 9781503816527
LCCN 2016945628

Printed in the United States of America
PA02324

## ABOUT THE AUTHOR

M. J. York is a writer and editor
from Minnesota. She enjoys spring
rains and planting her garden.

# Contents

# Helping Earth

It is Earth Day! We do things to help Earth.

Earth Day is April 22. We clean up our **community**. We pick up trash.

We plant a tree. It will be a home for birds and animals.

Cars cause **pollution**. We walk or bike instead.

# Save and Recycle

We save water. We turn it off when we brush our teeth.

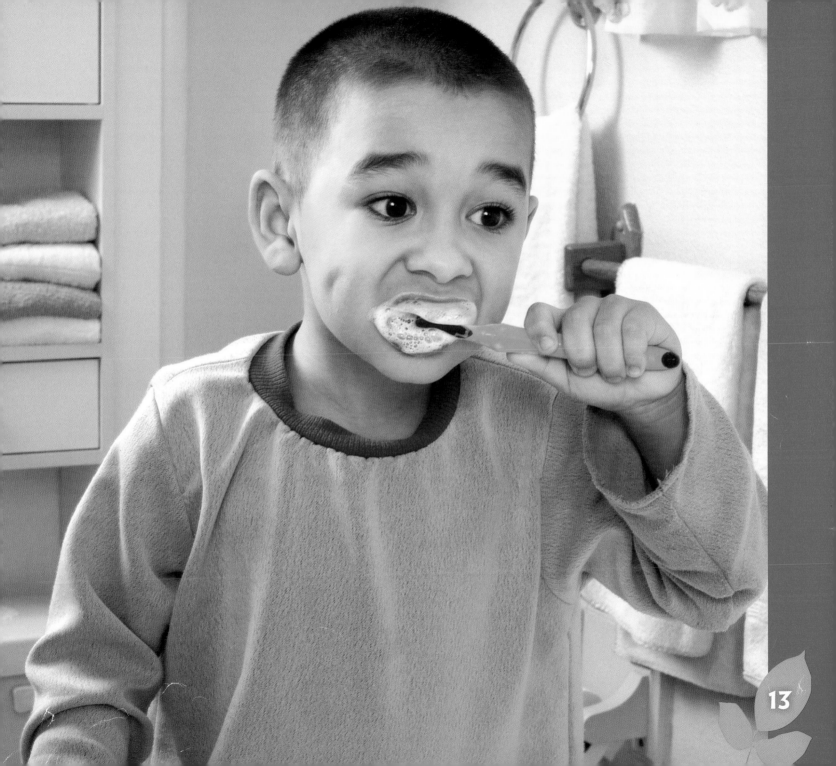

13

We **recycle** paper, glass, and plastic. We sort them out from the trash.

# Learning and Making

We read a book. We learn how to help Earth. We teach others what we learn.

We make a birdhouse.

Birds will come to nest.

We go outside. We walk in a park. We celebrate Earth Day every day!

# Make a Bird Feeder

Make your own bird feeder to watch birds come and eat!

**Supplies:**

| | |
|---|---|
| peanut butter | shoebox |
| toilet paper roll | birdseed |
| plastic knife | a long piece of string |

**Instructions:**

1. Use a plastic knife to spread peanut butter on the toilet paper roll.
2. Pour birdseed in the shoebox. Roll the toilet paper roll in the birdseed.
3. Thread the string through the hole in the toilet paper roll.
4. Hang it outside where you can see it. Watch for birds or squirrels that come to eat!

# Glossary

**community** — (kuh-MYOO-ni-tee) A community is a place and the people who live there. I help keep my community clean.

**pollution** — (puh-LOO-shun) Pollution is something that harms or dirties the air, water, or soil. We try to make less pollution.

**recycle** — (ree-SYE-kul) To recycle is to turn old materials such as glass, paper, metal, or plastic into new things. We sort out items from the trash that we want to recycle.

# To Learn More

## Books

Inches, Alison. *I Can Save the Earth!*
New York, NY: Little Simon, 2008.

McNamara, Margaret. *Earth Day.*
New York, NY: Aladdin, 2009.

Parr, Todd. *The EARTH Book*. New York,
NY: Little, Brown, 2010.

## Web Sites

Visit our Web site for links about
Earth Day: **childsworld.com/links**

Note to Parents, Teachers, and Librarians: We routinely verify
our Web links to make sure they are safe and active sites. So
encourage your readers to check them out!

# Index

24